Estimating Flow-Duration and Low-Flow Frequency Statistics for Unregulated Streams in Oregon

By John Risley, Adam Stonewall, and Tana Haluska

Prepared in cooperation with the Oregon Department of Transportation

Scientific Investigations Report 2008–5126

U.S. Department of the Interior
U.S. Geological Survey

DISCLAIMER

This document is disseminated under the sponsorship of the Oregon Department of Transportation and the United States Department of Transportation in the interest of information exchange. The State of Oregon and the United States Government assume no liability of its contents or use thereof.

The contents of this report reflect the view of the authors who are solely responsible for the facts and accuracy of the material presented. The contents do not necessarily reflect the official views of the Oregon Department of Transportation or the United States Department of Transportation.

The State of Oregon and the United States Government do not endorse products of manufacturers. Trademarks or manufacturers' names appear herein only because they are considered essential to the object of this document.

This report does not constitute a standard, specification, or regulation.

Technical Report Documentation Page

1. Report No. FHWA-OR-RD-09-03	2. Government Accession No.	3. Recipient's Catalog No.
4. Title and Subtitle Estimating Flow-Duration and Low-Flow Frequency Statistics for Unregulated Streams in Oregon		5. Report Date August 2008
		6. Performing Organization Code
7. Author(s) John Risley (US Geological Survey) Adam Stonewall (US Geological Survey) Tana Haluska (US Geological Survey)		8. Performing Organization Report No.
9. Performing Organization Name and Address Oregon Department of Transportation Research Unit 200 Hawthorne Ave. SE, Suite B-240 Salem, OR 97301-5192		10. Work Unit No. (TRAIS)
		11. Contract or Grant No. SPR 637
12. Sponsoring Agency Name and Address Oregon Department of Transportation Research Unit and 200 Hawthorne Ave. SE, Suite B-240 Salem, OR 97301-5192 Federal Highway Administration 400 Seventh Street, SW Washington, DC 20590-0003		13. Type of Report and Period Covered Final Report
		14. Sponsoring Agency Code
15. Supplementary Notes		

16. Abstract

Flow statistical datasets, basin-characteristic datasets, and regression equations were developed to provide decision makers with surface-water information needed for activities such as water-quality regulation, water-rights adjudication, biological habitat assessment, infrastructure design, and water-supply planning and management. The flow statistics, which included annual and monthly period of record flow durations (5th, 10th, 25th, 50th, and 95th percent exceedances) and annual and monthly 7-day, 10-year (7Q10) and 7-day, 2-year (7Q2) low flows, were computed at 466 streamflow-gaging stations at sites with unregulated flow conditions throughout Oregon and adjacent areas of neighboring States. Regression equations, created from the flow statistics and basin characteristics of the stations, can be used to estimate flow statistics at ungaged stream sites in Oregon. The study area was divided into 10 regression modeling regions based on ecological, topographic, geologic, hydrologic, and climatic criteria. In total, 910 annual and monthly regression equations were created to predict the 7 flow statistics in the 10 regions. Equations to predict the five flow-duration exceedance percentages and the two low-flow frequency statistics were created with Ordinary Least Squares and Generalized Least Squares regression, respectively. The standard errors of estimate of the equations created to predict the 5th and 95th percent exceedances had medians of 42.4 and 64.4 percent, respectively. The standard errors of prediction of the equations created to predict the 7Q2 and 7Q10 low-flow statistics had medians of 51.7 and 61.2 percent, respectively. Standard errors for regression equations for sites in western Oregon were smaller than those in eastern Oregon partly because of a greater density of available streamflow-gaging stations in western Oregon than eastern Oregon. High-flow regression equations (such as the 5th and 10th percent exceedances) also generally were more accurate than the low-flow regression equations (such as the 95th percent exceedance and 7Q10 low-flow statistic). The regression equations predict unregulated flow conditions in Oregon. Flow estimates need to be adjusted if they are used at ungaged sites that are regulated by reservoirs or affected by water-supply and agricultural withdrawals if actual flow conditions are of interest. The regression equations are installed in the USGS StreamStats Web-based tool (http://water.usgs.gov/osw/streamstats/index.html, accessed July 16, 2008). StreamStats provides users with a set of annual and monthly flow-duration and low-flow frequency estimates for ungaged sites in Oregon in addition to the basin characteristics for the sites. Prediction intervals at the 90-percent confidence level also are automatically computed.

17. Key Words stream, flow, statistics, low-flow, regression		18. Distribution Statement Copies available from NTIS, and online at http://www.oregon.gov/ODOT/TD/TP_RES/	
19. Security Classification (of this report) Unclassified	20. Security Classification (of this page) Unclassified	21. No. of Pages 22	22. Price

Technical Report Form DOT F 1700.7 (8-72)   Reproduction of completed page authorized   ♻ Printed on recycled paper

U.S. Department of the Interior
DIRK KEMPTHORNE, Secretary

U.S. Geological Survey
Mark D. Myers, Director

U.S. Geological Survey, Reston, Virginia: 2008

Contents

Figures

Tables

Conversion Factors and Datums

Conversion Factors

Multiply	By	To obtain
inch (in.)	2.54	centimeter (cm)
foot (ft)	0.3048	meter (m)
mile (mi)	1.609	kilometer (km)
acre	0.4047	hectare (ha)
square mile (mi^2)	2.590	square kilometer (km^2)
cubic foot per second (ft^3/s)	0.02832	cubic meter per second (m^3/s)
inch per year (in/yr)	25.4	millimeter per year (mm/yr)
inch per hour (in/hr)	25.4	millimeter per hour (mm/hr)

Temperature in degrees Fahrenheit (°F) may be converted to degrees Celsius (°C) as follows:

$$°C=(°F-32)/1.8.$$

Datums

Vertical coordinate information is referenced to the North American Vertical Datum of 1988 (NAVD 88).

Horizontal coordinate information is referenced to the North American Datum of 1983 (NAD 83).

Altitude, as used in this report, refers to distance above the vertical datum.

This page intentionally left blank

Estimating Flow-Duration and Low-Flow Frequency Statistics for Unregulated Streams in Oregon

By John Risley, Adam Stonewall, and Tana Haluska

Abstract

Flow statistical datasets, basin-characteristic datasets, and regression equations were developed to provide decision makers with surface-water information needed for activities such as water-quality regulation, water-rights adjudication, biological habitat assessment, infrastructure design, and water-supply planning and management. The flow statistics, which included annual and monthly period of record flow durations (5th, 10th, 25th, 50th, and 95th percent exceedances) and annual and monthly 7-day, 10-year (7Q10) and 7-day, 2-year (7Q2) low flows, were computed at 466 streamflow-gaging stations at sites with unregulated flow conditions throughout Oregon and adjacent areas of neighboring States. Regression equations, created from the flow statistics and basin characteristics of the stations, can be used to estimate flow statistics at ungaged stream sites in Oregon. The study area was divided into 10 regression modeling regions based on ecological, topographic, geologic, hydrologic, and climatic criteria. In total, 910 annual and monthly regression equations were created to predict the 7 flow statistics in the 10 regions. Equations to predict the five flow-duration exceedance percentages and the two low-flow frequency statistics were created with Ordinary Least Squares and Generalized Least Squares regression, respectively. The standard errors of estimate of the equations created to predict the 5th and 95th percent exceedances had medians of 42.4 and 64.4 percent, respectively. The standard errors of prediction of the equations created to predict the 7Q2 and 7Q10 low-flow statistics had medians of 51.7 and 61.2 percent, respectively.

Standard errors for regression equations for sites in western Oregon were smaller than those in eastern Oregon partly because of a greater density of available streamflow-gaging stations in western Oregon than eastern Oregon. High-flow regression equations (such as the 5th and 10th percent exceedances) also generally were more accurate than the low-flow regression equations (such as the 95th percent exceedance and 7Q10 low-flow statistic).

The regression equations predict unregulated flow conditions in Oregon. Flow estimates need to be adjusted if they are used at ungaged sites that are regulated by reservoirs or affected by water-supply and agricultural withdrawals if actual flow conditions are of interest.

The regression equations are installed in the USGS StreamStats Web-based tool (http://water.usgs.gov/osw/streamstats/index.html, accessed July 16, 2008). StreamStats provides users with a set of annual and monthly flow-duration and low-flow frequency estimates for ungaged sites in Oregon in addition to the basin characteristics for the sites. Prediction intervals at the 90-percent confidence level also are automatically computed.

Introduction

Between 2005 and 2040, the population of Oregon is expected to increase by about 1.8 million (http://www.oregon.gov/DAS/OEA/popsurvey.shtml, accessed July 16, 2008). As a consequence of projected population growth in urban and rural locations, competition over water resources in the State could become more profound. In many locations within Oregon, water supplies are already insufficient to meet the needs of aquatic habitat, agricultural irrigation, industry, and urban drinking-water consumption. To meet future challenges, improved information-based tools are needed to better characterize and manage water resources.

Flow statistics can be used to characterize flow of a certain magnitude at a location of interest on a stream. Flow statistics are crucial to Federal, State, and local agencies for water-quality regulatory activities and water-supply planning and management. These statistics are used as benchmarks when setting wastewater-treatment plant effluent limits and allowable pollutant loads to meet water-quality standards. Hundreds of river reaches in Oregon have been designated as impaired (exceeding water-quality and/or biological criteria) by Total Maximum Daily Load (TMDL) assessments.

Reliable estimates of expected streamflow are needed at specific periods of the year when determining the maximum allowable load of a pollutant. Aside from water-quality regulatory activities, flow statistics are used in design and management decisions for hydroelectric facilities, reservoir storage, fish passage, stream restoration, temporary control of water during construction, culverts, bridges, and agricultural irrigation systems. Low-flow statistics, in particular, are used in water-use permit decisions and the adjudication of water conflicts between competing users. Low-flow statistics also are increasingly being used in ecological research. Low-flow conditions can create biological responses and changes in habitat such as reduced population size of aquatic species and shifts in the quantity of species type.

An accurate calculation of flow statistics is dependent on the availability and quantity of measured flow records on a stream. The U.S. Geological Survey (USGS), Oregon Water Resources Department (OWRD), and other public agencies operate continuous streamflow-gaging stations in Oregon and surrounding States that provide flow data needed for various purposes. Although flow statistics can be calculated at these locations, techniques can be used to make estimates of flow statistics at locations where streamflow-gaging stations do not exist. If the stream location where a flow statistic is needed is close to a gaging station then streamflow information can be extrapolated from the gaging-station record. For locations farther away from gaging stations, regression equations that relate flow statistics with physical and climatic characteristics of drainage basins can be used.

Regression equations for estimating flow statistics were developed for use in Oregon and are described in this report. In addition, the regressions equations developed from this study also are included in the USGS StreamStats Web-based tool (http://water.usgs.gov/osw/streamstats/index.html, accessed July 16, 2008). StreamStats allows users to obtain flow statistics, drainage-basin characteristics, and other information for user-selected sites on a stream. Using a GIS-based interactive map of Oregon, the user can 'point and click' on a location and StreamStats will rapidly delineate the basin upstream of the selected location. The user also can 'point and click' on USGS streamflow-gaging stations and receive flow statistics and information about those stations.

Purpose and Scope

This report presents the results of statistical analyses used to compute period of record annual and monthly flow duration and low-flow frequency statistics at unregulated sites throughout Oregon. These statistics include flow durations (5th, 10th, 25th, 50th, and 95th percent exceedances) and the 7-day, 10-year (7Q10) and 7-day, 2-year (7Q2) low flows. In addition to providing methods for calculating flow duration

and low-flow frequency statistics from streamflow records, the report also describes the development of regression equations that relate basin physical and climatic characteristics to flow statistics. These equations provide estimates of unregulated flow conditions at locations where streamflow data are unavailable (ungaged sites). The report also provides a discussion of the accuracy and limitations of the flow statistics and regression equations.

Description of Study Area

The equations for estimating flow statistics were developed for use only in Oregon. The equations were developed from flow statistics and basin characteristics at streamflow-gaging stations in Oregon and adjacent areas of the neighboring States of Washington, Idaho, Nevada, and California. The study area includes a wide range of geologic, physiographic, biological, and climatic characteristics. The area contains all or portions of nine U.S. Environmental Protection Agency (EPA) Level III ecoregions: *Coast Range, Klamath Mountains, Willamette Valley, Cascades, Eastern Cascades Slopes and Foothills, Columbia Plateau, Blue Mountains, Snake River Plain,* and *Northern Basin and Range* (U.S. Environmental Protection Agency, 1996) (fig. 1). These ecoregions were initially used as the basis for grouping streamflow-gaging stations for the development of the flow statistics regression equations. Ecoregion boundaries were adjusted to provide hydrologic regions within which various sets of regression equations were applicable as discussed in section, "Modeling Regions."

In western Oregon, the *Coast Range* ecoregion separates the Pacific Ocean and the *Willamette Valley* ecoregion. Altitudes in the *Coast Range* are relatively low compared to other mountainous regions of Oregon. Major river basins in the *Coast Range* include the Nehalem, Siletz, Siuslaw, and parts of the Umpqua, which all drain to the Pacific Ocean. The ecoregion is dominated by lush conifer rain forests composed of Sitka Spruce, Western Hemlock, and Douglas Fir. Mean annual precipitation typically ranges from 80 to 100 in. High-altitude areas can get more than 200 in/yr of precipitation (http://www.ocs.oregonstate.edu/index.html, accessed July 16, 2008). Although winters are wetter than summers, air temperatures are mild and nearly constant year round at many locations.

The *Klamath Mountains* ecoregion is in southwestern Oregon. In the Oregon portion of this ecoregion, most runoff drains from the Rogue River basin into the Pacific Ocean. Mean annual precipitation in the western side of the *Klamath Mountains*, close to the Pacific Ocean, typically ranges from 80 to 100 in. However, areas to the east, around Medford and Ashland, typically receive only 20 in/yr of precipitation. Natural vegetation includes Oregon White Oak, Douglas Fir, and Ponderosa Pine.

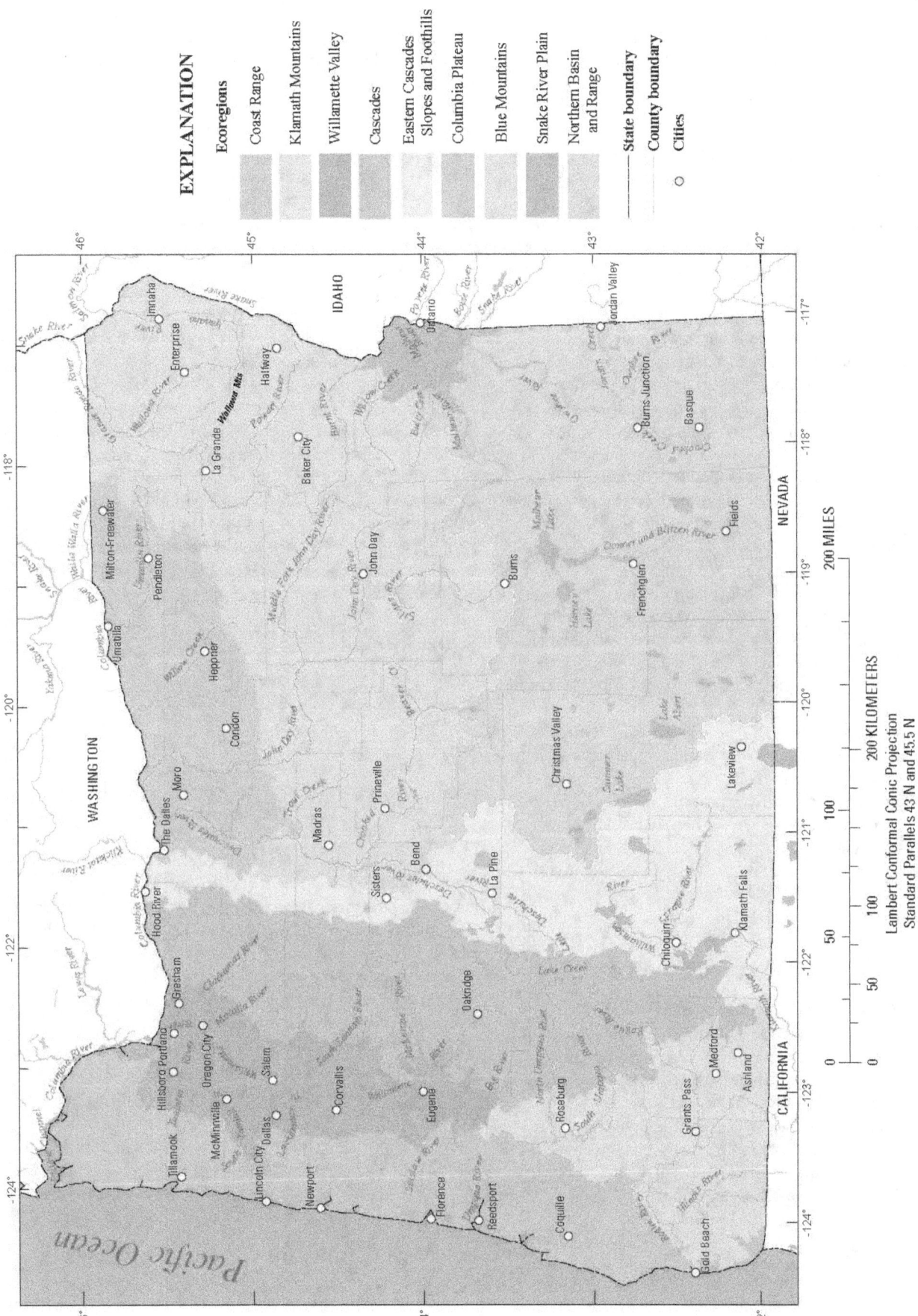

Figure 1. Level III ecoregions of Oregon.

Most of the *Willamette Valley* ecoregion is contained within the Willamette River basin. Runoff flows from the Willamette River into the Columbia River before it reaches the Pacific Ocean. Composed of flood alluvial material, the *Willamette Valley* is fairly flat and gently slopes from south to north. Altitudes near Eugene are around 500 ft and at sea level near Portland. Mean annual precipitation ranges from 40 to 50 in. About 80 percent of annual precipitation falls between October and May. Summers in the *Willamette Valley* can be hot and dry. Natural vegetation at high altitudes is dominated by Douglas Firs and other conifers. Oregon White Oak, Douglas Fir, ashes, alder, and maples are more common in low altitudes.

The *Cascades* ecoregion is immediately to the east of the *Willamette Valley*. As part of a larger mountain range extending from British Columbia to California, the *Cascades* are a natural north-south dividing line between western and eastern Oregon. Mean annual precipitation can be more than 140 in. at high altitudes. Several peaks in the region are glaciated and at altitudes of more than 10,000 ft. Natural vegetation in the *Cascades* is dominated by conifers such as Douglas Fir, Western Hemlock, and Western redcedar. The *Cascades* are composed mostly of highly permeable volcanic materials. As a consequence, many streams are spring fed and have a near constant discharge throughout most of the year (Manga, 1996). The *Cascades* contain the headwaters of the Clackamas, Santiam, and McKenzie Rivers, all of which flow into the Willamette River. The *Cascades* also include the headwaters of the Umpqua and Rogue Rivers, tributaries of the Pacific Ocean.

The *Eastern Cascades Slopes and Foothills* ecoregion extending from Washington to California contains snowmelt fed streams flowing eastward off of the *Cascades* into the Deschutes or Klamath River basins. This ecoregion is noteworthy for its numerous and highly productive spring fed streams, which includes the Metolius River, Fall River, Wood River, Annie Creek, Spring Creek, and Sheep Creek. The *Eastern Cascades Slopes and Foothills* ecoregion is in the rainshadow of the Cascades and receives significantly less precipitation ranging from about 20 to 50 in/yr. Natural vegetation in this ecoregion contains open stands of Ponderosa and Lodgepole Pine.

The *Columbia Plateau* ecoregion in north-central Oregon contains the Umatilla River basin in addition to the lower portions of the Deschutes and John Day River basins. This region drains the north side of the Blue Mountains and slopes from the south from an altitude of about 3,000 ft to a few hundred feet above sea level along the Columbia River in the north. Like much of eastern Oregon, annual precipitation in this region is less than 20 in/yr. The natural landscape is dominated mostly by grasslands and sagebrush.

The *Blue Mountains* ecoregion dominates northeastern Oregon. As the wettest ecoregion in eastern Oregon, conifer forests and alpine vegetation are present at high altitudes. The Wallowa Mountains on the eastern side of the *Blue Mountains* have several peaks more than 9,000 ft in altitude with a mean annual precipitation greater than 70 in. Runoff in the western side of the *Blue Mountains* flows into the Deschutes or the John Day Rivers and then into the Columbia River. Runoff in the eastern side drains into the Grand Ronde or the Powder Rivers and then into the Snake River.

A small portion of eastern Oregon is in the *Snake River Plain* ecoregion. Mean annual precipitation generally is less than 12 in/yr. Natural vegetation is dominated by grasslands and sagebrush. The limited runoff generated in this region flows into the Malheur and Snake Rivers.

Southeastern Oregon is a part of the *Northern Basin and Range* ecoregion. This ecoregion has few perennial streams and contains some of the driest areas of the State. The natural landscape is characterized by grasslands, creosote, and sagebrush. Mean annual precipitation in the Alvord Desert is less than 4 in. Most basins in this part of Oregon have no outlet to the sea and are within the Great Basin of the Western United States. Runoff in the closed basins terminates at existing or dried-up lakes. The largest of these lakes include Malheur, Abert, Harney, and Summer.

Previous Studies

Lystrom (1970) published a statewide [Oregon] evaluation of low-flow characteristics that included low-flow equations. Equations for determining water availability in Oregon are provided in Cooper (2002). Harris and others (1979) developed regression equations for predicting peak discharges in rural unregulated streams in western Oregon. Harris and Hubbard (1983) developed peak-discharge regression equations for eastern Oregon. Using additional years of data and streamflow sites, Cooper (2005; 2006) developed peak-discharge regression equations for streams in western and eastern Oregon, respectively. In the 1960s, the USGS published a series of Water-Supply Papers analyzing the magnitude and frequency of floods throughout the continental United States. Publications from the series that included portions of Oregon are Thomas and others (1963), Hulsing and Kallio (1964), Butler and others (1966), and Young and Cruff (1967). Portions of southern Oregon also were included in a flood regionalization study by Thomas and others (1993).

Calculating Flow-Duration and Low-Flow Frequency Statistics at Streamflow-Gaging Stations

Historical flow data collected at continuous streamflow-gaging stations, sufficient in quality and quantity, are fundamental to the accurate calculation of flow statistics. All data used to compute flow statistics in this study were from daily mean flow records at streamflow-gaging stations operated by the USGS or OWRD in Oregon and from streamflow-gaging stations operated by the USGS in the neighboring States of Washington, Idaho, Nevada, and California. Flow statistics based on daily flow data can be used as benchmarks for planners and water managers who may need to determine if streamflow will be sufficient for water-quality and aquatic habitat needs, or if streamflows will exceed the design capacity of a reservoir or a bridge.

Flow Duration

Flow-duration data commonly are used to statistically characterize streamflow. Flow-duration data are daily mean flow values measured over a specified time interval that have been exceeded various percentages of the specified time interval. For example, a 5-percent exceedance probability represents a high flow that has been exceeded only 5-percent of all days of the flow record. Conversely, a 95-percent exceedance probability would characterize low-flow conditions in a stream, because 95 percent of all daily mean flows in the record are greater than that amount.

For flow-duration statistics to be reliable indicators of probable future conditions, a minimum of 10 years of record typically is used (Searcy, 1959). The equation used to compute the exceedance probability, which also is referred to as the flow-duration percentile, is given as:

$$P = 100 * (m/(n+1))\qquad(1)$$

where
  P is the exceedance probability,
  m is the ranking, from highest to lowest, of all daily mean flows for the specified period of record, and
  n is the total number of daily mean flows.

To determine the flow for a specific flow duration percentile, interpolation between the discharges associated with percentiles on either side of the specific percentile may be needed. Flows that are equal to each other also would be given separate m rank values. With the equation above, high flows are assigned low percentiles and low flows are assigned high percentiles. This is contrary to the computation of nonexceedance flow duration percentiles used in some statistical software packages, where high and low flows correspond to high and low percentiles, respectively.

Low-Flow Frequency

The 7-day, 2-year (7Q2) and 10-year (7Q10) annual low-flow statistics are based on an annual series of the smallest values of mean discharge computed over any 7-consecutive days during the annual period. A probability distribution is fit to the annual series of 7-day minimums, and the 7Q2 statistic is the annual 7-day minimum flow with a 2-year recurrence interval (nonexceedance probability of 50 percent), although the 7Q10 statistic is the annual 7-day minimum flow with a 10-year recurrence interval (nonexceedance probability of 10 percent). Low-flow frequency also can be computed on a seasonal or monthly basis by limiting the daily data used for the annual series to just the season or month of interest. For example, the March 7Q2 and 7Q10 flow statistics are calculated by fitting a probability distribution to the annual series of 7-day minimums computed just from daily mean flows in March of every year.

The log-Pearson Type III probability distribution (U.S. Interagency Advisory Committee on Water Data, 1982), which typically is used for determining low-flow frequencies, was used for determining low-flow frequency for this study. An overview of techniques used to compute low-flow frequency statistics is provided by Riggs (1972), and more specific information about the log-Pearson Type III distribution can be found in a report by the U.S. Interagency Advisory Committee on Water Data (1982). The climatic year (April 1 to March 31) was used to define the starting and ending dates of annual periods for computation of the 7-day minimum flows. Although most annual 7-day low flows occur during the summer months, the annual 7-day low flow can sometimes occur in the winter during prolonged subfreezing periods at high-altitude streamflow-gaging stations. The annual 7-day low flows at some streamflow-gaging stations used in this study were equal to zero. A conditional probability adjustment for zero flow values (U.S. Interagency Advisory Committee on Water Data, 1982, appendix 5) was used for sites with one or more annual 7-day low-flow values of zero.

Although flow-duration and low-flow frequency statistics commonly are computed on an annual basis, they also can be computed on a seasonal or monthly basis. For example, the 7Q10 flow for March would be calculated using just daily mean flows for every March for the period of record.

Estimating Flow-Duration and Low-Flow-Frequency Statistics at Ungaged Stream Sites

Flow-duration and low-flow frequency statistics can be estimated at ungaged stream sites using several methods that include (1) a drainage-area ratio relation, (2) use of miscellaneous flow measurements at the ungaged site (commonly termed a partial-record site), and (3) a regional regression equation.

Drainage-Area Ratio Method

The drainage-area ratio method is the preferred method for estimating low-flow statistics at an ungaged site on a stream with gaged record. However, the method generally is reliable only if the ungaged site is close to the gaged site (also know as an index station). This method is based on the assumption that the unit area runoff of the ungaged basin is the same as that for the gaged site. The equation used in this method is as follows:

$$Q_u = [DA_u / DA_g] * Q_g \qquad (2)$$

where

Q_u is the low-flow statistic of the ungaged site,

DA_u is the drainage area of the ungaged site,

DA_g is the drainage area of the gaged site, and

Q_g is the low-flow statistic of the gaged site.

This method is often used when the ungaged site is on the same stream, upstream or downstream, of the gaged site and the drainage-area ratio of the two sites is between 0.5 and 1.5. This range of ratios has been confirmed in flood-frequency analyses in Montana (Parrett and Johnson, 2004) and Idaho (Kjelstrom, 1998; Berenbrock, 2002). Ries and Friesz (2000) determined that a range of 0.3 to 1.5 was appropriate for low-flow statistics in Massachusetts.

Partial-Record Site Method

At a partial-record site, a series of miscellaneous streamflow measurements are collected during low-flow conditions over a period of several years. These measurements, typically a minimum of 10, are then used to develop a graphical or statistical relation with concurrent daily mean flows at nearby streamflow-gaging stations (index stations). The relation can be determined by plotting partial-record flows against flows from an index station site. Often the curve, or lack of curve, and the visual correlation of the plot can determine the appropriate method to use for estimating the low-flow statistic at the partial-record site. Riggs (1972) provides details for using the graphical estimation method. After the low-flow statistic for the index station has been plotted on the curve, the corresponding low-flow statistic for the partial-record site can be estimated by drawing a straight line from the plotted point on the curve to the partial-record site axis. Ordinary Least Squares (OLS) regression can be used to estimate the low-flow statistic for the partial-record site by fitting a line between the concurrent flow points of the partial-record site and index station. However, OLS will create a low-flow estimate that is biased because the variances of the concurrent flow measurements for the partial-record site and index station are not equal. To avoid this bias, many low-flow analyses have used the Maintenance Of Variance Extension technique (MOVE.1 and MOVE.2) (Hirsch, 1982) or the base-flow correlation method (Stedinger and Thomas, 1985). Other techniques to remove bias include MOVE.3 and MOVE.4 (Vogel and Stedinger, 1985) and the GMOVE technique (Grygier and others, 1989).

Regression Equation Method

Linear multiple regression analysis is another method of estimating streamflow statistics at ungaged sites. Multiple regression is used to create equations that relate streamflow statistics of gaged sites in a region with the climatic and physical characteristics of their upstream drainage areas. Once an optimal equation has been determined, a streamflow statistic at an ungaged site can then be estimated using the relevant basin characteristics of the ungaged site.

The equation describing a linear multiple regression analysis is:

$$Y_i = b_o + b_1 X_1 + b_2 X_2 + \dots + b_n X_n + e_i \qquad (3)$$

where

Y_i is the dependent variable (estimated streamflow statistic) for site i,

b_o to b_n are the regression model coefficients determined in the analysis,

X_1 to X_n are the independent variable (basin characteristics) for site i,

e_i is the residual error or difference between the observed and estimated dependent variable for site i.

Linear regression analysis is based on the following assumptions: (1) the mean of the residuals (e_i) is zero, (2) the variance of the residuals is constant, (3) the residuals are normally distributed, and (4) the residuals are independent of each other. In addition to these assumptions, the selected independent variables (X) should have a good physical basis as predictors of the streamflow statistic. The plus and minus terms of the equation should make hydrological sense. For example, a variable such as drainage area should have a positive coefficient because an increase in drainage area should result in an increase in the streamflow statistic. The independent variables in the equation also should not be strongly correlated with each other.

In almost all regionalization studies, low-flow and peak-flow statistics, the dependent and independent datasets are skewed. As a consequence, the data needs to be transformed in order to satisfy the first assumption of having the mean of the residuals equal zero. In many studies, a logarithmic transformation is used. A base$_{10}$ log-transformed multiple regression equation has the form of:

$$\log Y_i = b_o + b_1 \log X_1 + b_2 \log X_2 + \dots + b_n \log X_n + e_i \qquad (4)$$

After the coefficients have been determined through regression analysis, the equation is transformed back to its original units in a form that can be used to estimate a specific streamflow statistic at an ungaged site. The retransformed equation has the following form:

$$Y_i = 10^{b_o} X_1^{b_1} X_2^{b_2} \dots X_n^{b_n} 10^{e_i} \qquad (5)$$

A linear regression equation provides an unbiased estimate of the mean response of the dependent variable. Although estimates provided by equation 4 are unbiased, these estimates are in log units and estimates in the original units are needed. Estimates from equation 5 are in the original units. However, this equation predicts the median, instead of the mean, response of the dependent variable. A streamflow statistic based on a median response creates an estimate that is biased and tends to be lower than the mean (Ries and Friesz, 2000). Bias correction factors (BCF) have been used in some studies to remove the bias from the estimate (Ries, 1994; Ries and Friesz, 2000; Flynn, 2003). The specific BCFs that were used in this study are discussed in section, "Bias Correction Factors."

In regression analysis, a least-squares method can be used to estimate the equation coefficients. The coefficients are determined after minimizing the sum of the squared differences of the measured and predicted Y values. Ordinary-least-squares (OLS) regression assumes that each data vector in the analysis is providing equal information to the equation. All data vectors are then given an equal weight in determining the equation coefficients through minimizing the sum of the squared errors. In a flow regionalization study, streamflow-gaging stations (data vectors) are not providing equal information because streamflow statistics computed from stations with long records generally are more accurate than those computed from stations with short records. The stations also are not entirely independent from each other even though independence is one of the assumptions of linear regression analysis. Station flow records are sometimes spatially correlated because of similar climatic and physical basin characteristics. High spatial correlation can result in an over-representation of information from those stations. Weighted-least-squares (WLS) and generalized-least-squares (GLS) regression are two methods used to provide an appropriate weight for each data vector (streamflow-gaging station) in the analysis. Tasker (1980) developed a WLS method for peak-flow and low-flow frequency applications that computes weights based on the flow-record length and the variance of the annual peak flows or 7-day low flows of each streamflow-gaging station. The GLS method computes station weights based on record length, variance, and spatial cross-correlation (Tasker and Stedinger, 1989). The application of the GLS method in this study is discussed in more detail in section, "Generalized Least Squares Regression Analysis."

Development of Regression Equations for Estimating Flow-Duration and Low-Flow-Frequency Statistics in Oregon

Developing regression equations to estimate flow-duration and low-flow frequency statistics throughout Oregon involved a rigorous process of data screening, selection of streamflow-gaging stations, and computation of streamflow statistics and drainage-basin characteristics for each station, and regression analysis. Because unique equations were needed for each streamflow statistic for annual and monthly periods and for different regions of the study area, a total of 910 equations were developed from 466 streamflow-gaging stations.

Streamflow Data Screening

More than 1,100 active and discontinued streamflow-gaging stations in Oregon, Washington, Idaho, Nevada, and California were evaluated for this study. Although most of these stations were or are operated by the USGS, some stations operated by OWRD also were included. After being assessed for quality, the non-USGS stations were included in the analysis to increase the spatial density of stations that was needed in some areas of the State.

Streamflow-gaging stations were selected using the following criteria:

1. A minimum of 10 years of flow record.

2. No regulation, flow augmentation, or water-supply/industrial withdrawals in the upstream drainage basin.

3. A stationary (no trends over time) flow record.

This study, like other USGS regional regression studies, used a minimum of 10 years of flow record for streamflow-gaging station selection (Ries and Friez, 2000; Berenbrock, 2002; Flynn, 2003; Cooper, 2005; and Hortness, 2006). Minimum record lengths of 20 or 30 years of flow record would have provided a broader representation of climate variability in the study area. However, using a longer minimum record length would have decreased the number of available streamflow-gaging stations in regions of the study that already had limited data coverage.

The drainage basins of the streamflow-gaging stations with 10 or more years of record were assessed for anthropogenic impacts that alter the hydrologic flow regime. Reservoirs typically modulate flow regimes by reducing flood peaks and augmenting summer low flows. If a significant upstream reservoir were in existence during the entire period of a flow record, then the streamflow-gaging station was not included in the study. However, stations with at least 10 years of flow record that predated the construction of a reservoir were included. Streamflow-gaging stations also were eliminated if significant inter-basin water transfers, industrial and urban wastewater flow augmentation, and/or urban water-supply withdrawals occurred in their upstream drainage basins. However, station flow records for sites in Oregon where agricultural irrigation withdrawals occurred were included in the study. A methodology used to account for agricultural consumptive use losses is discussed in section, "Consumptive-Use Adjustments." A rigorous effort was made to eliminate streamflow-gaging stations with flow records that had been significantly impacted by anthropogenic activities. However, there exists the possibility that some of the flow records selected for the study contained some unaccounted anthropogenic impacts. A comprehensive analysis of all anthropogenic hydrologic impacts in more than 1,100 drainage basins would have been a monumental undertaking and was not within the scope of the study.

In the final stage of data selection, flow records of the streamflow-gaging stations were analyzed for significant trends in flow over time (nonstationarity). In frequency analysis, annual peak floods or low flows are assumed to be independent and stationary over time. Annual time series that are nonstationary are not independent and are thus not suitable for frequency analysis. Trends in flow records can result from anthropogenic causes such as changes in land use in the drainage basins above gaging stations or from long-term climate cycles. Trends in some records, particularly short-term records, also may be a result of decadal climate variability that would not be significant in longer records. An analysis of the precipitation record (1932–2005) at Crater Lake National Park, for example, showed decadal-scale drought cycles (Gannett and others, 2007). Although select 10- or 20-year periods within this record would likely contain significant nonstationarity by themselves, the long-term Crater Lake precipitation record (1931–96) did not have significant trends (Risley and Laenen, 1999). All flow records with significant nonstationarity were not included in this study.

Most of the 7-day low-flow time series computed for the entire climate year (April 1 to March 31) and for each month were evaluated for nonstationarity using Kendall's *tau*. The Kendall's *tau* statistic indicates if there is a monotonically increasing or decreasing trend in the time-series data (Helsel and Hirsch, 2002). Because Kendall's *tau* is a nonparametric distribution-free test, there is no need for any *a priori* knowledge of distribution parameter values or form.

Flow records with more than one zero value in their 7-day time series were evaluated for nonstationarity using the Pearson correlation coefficient (Hirsch and others, 1993). Because the Pearson correlation coefficient assumes normally distributed dependent variables, it is not distribution free. Both the Kendall's *tau* and the Pearson correlation coefficient were applied as two-sided tests with a significance level of 5 percent.

After screening all available flow records, a total of 466 streamflow-gaging stations in Oregon and adjacent areas of neighboring States were selected (table 1 and fig. 2). The starting and ending years of the flow records all varied with the earliest starting 1891 and the most recent ending in water year 2005. Of the 466 streamflow-gaging stations, 88 were active and 378 were not active in 2005. Table 1 also shows the stations grouped into 10 regions. Separate sets of regression equations for the streamflow statistics were created for each region. The criteria that were used to group the stations are discussed in section, "Modeling Regions."

The period of record column in table 1 contains periods that were complete water years. These periods were used to compute the annual flow-duration and annual low-flow frequency statistics. However, many records contained additional incomplete years of flow data. To utilize all available flow data, the additional incomplete years in the form of complete months were added to the complete water-year periods and used to compute monthly streamflow statistics. As a consequence, the annual and monthly streamflow statistics for some stations are based on flow record periods all having slightly different starting and ending year periods (table 2). Not all of the 466 streamflow-gaging stations were included in every annual and monthly model in a region because the Kendall's *tau* and Pearson's tests for nonstationarity showed mixed results at many stations. For example, if the annual 7-day low-flow annual series of a station passed the Kendall's *tau* test, it would be included in the list of stations available for the annual models. However, if the January 7-day low-flow annual series for that same station failed the Kendall's *tau* test, then it would not be included in the January models.

Consumptive-Use Adjustments

An objective of the study was to provide estimates of flow-duration and low-flow frequency statistics of unregulated flow at gaged and ungaged sites throughout Oregon. Unregulated flow was defined as flow affected by reservoir operations as well as flow affected by all other anthropogenic effects including agricultural withdrawals. Using these criteria, the study provides estimates of more natural flow conditions in Oregon. Most of the 1,100 flow records initially available to the study had nonnatural flow conditions as a result of the effects of reservoir regulation, withdrawals, logging, etc. During the screening process, numerous flow records with known significant urban and industrial water supply

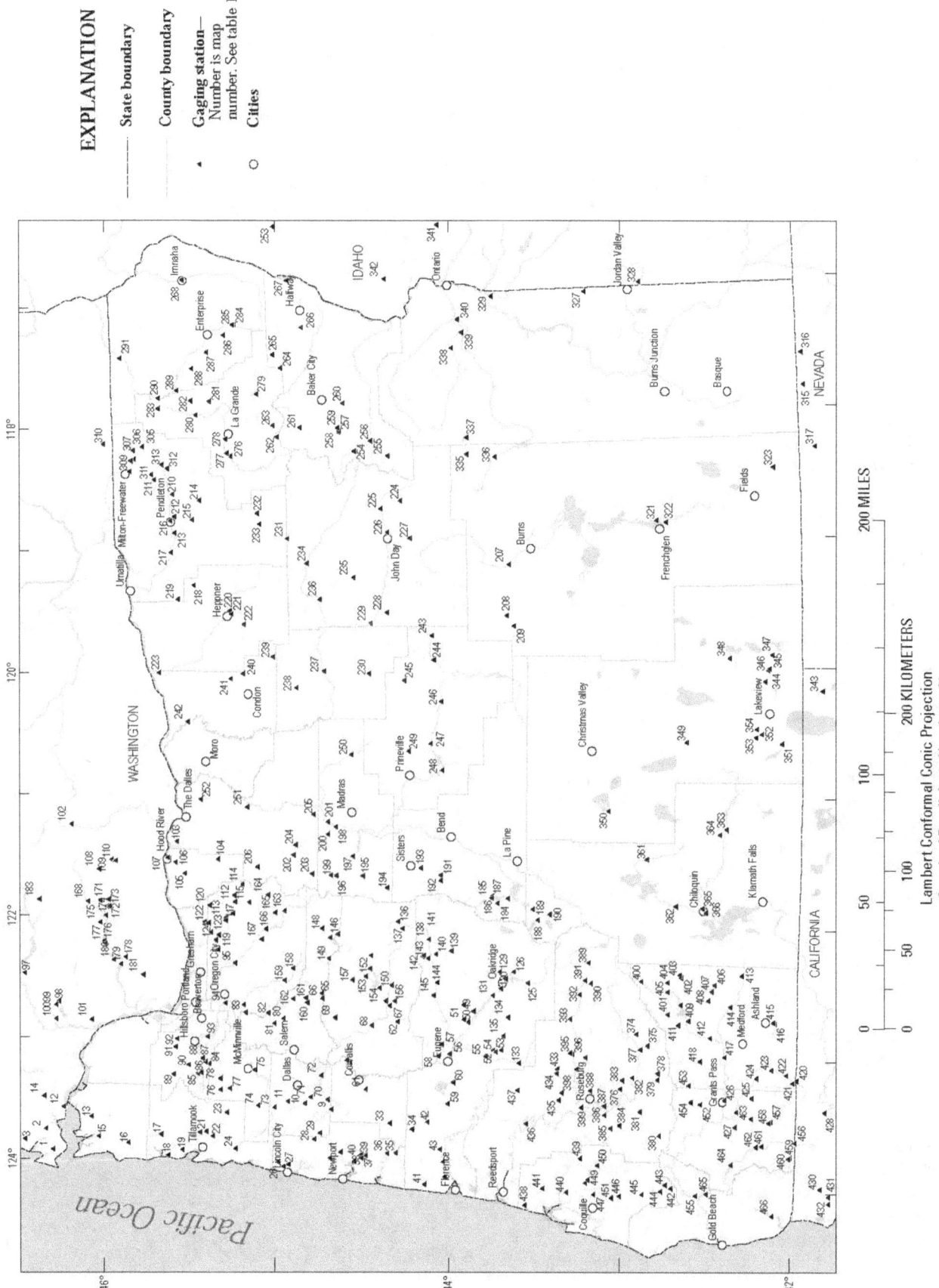

Figure 2.   Location of streamflow-gaging stations used in the regression equations. (Some streamflow-gaging stations listed in table 1, which are located in neighboring States, are not shown on the map.)

withdrawals in their drainage basins were eliminated from the study. However, eliminating all flow records with withdrawals for agricultural irrigation would have resulted in an insufficient density of streamflow-gaging stations in many regions of the study area. A decision was made to add estimates of monthly agricultural consumptive use to the daily flow records of stations in Oregon in order to represent near-natural flow conditions. Daily consumptive-use adjustments for each month were made to 254 of the 466 streamflow-gaging stations used in the study (table 3). The procedure used in this study to calculate the adjustments was developed by OWRD for their water availability analyses (Cooper, 2002). The procedure is described as follows:

1. Estimated total actual annual crop consumptive use for each 8-digit Hydrologic Unit Code (HUC) area within the entire study area was taken from Cooper (2002).

2. The total number of acres of land permitted for irrigation in the drainage basins of the streamflow-gaging stations was divided by the total number of acres of land permitted for irrigation within the 8-digit HUC. If a drainage basin was larger than a single HUC, a weighted ratio was computed. Data pertaining to the number of acres of land permitted for irrigation in both the drainage-areas of the streamflow-gaging stations and the HUCs was provided by OWRD (Richard M. Cooper, Oregon Water Resources Department, written commun. 2006).

3. Estimated actual annual crop consumptive use in the upstream drainage areas of the streamflow-gaging stations was determined by multiplying the ratio (from above) by the estimated total actual annual crop consumptive use in the HUC.

4. To estimate actual daily crop consumptive use (in cubic feet per second) for each month, the actual annual crop consumptive use volume was distributed over the months of the year using either of two methods. For regions in the State where sufficient water is available for irrigation throughout the growing season, the annual volume was multiplied by monthly fractions based on the theoretical crop water requirement for pasture developed by Cuenca and others (1992). For more arid regions of the State, the annual volume was multiplied by monthly fractions based on actual canal diversions (Cooper, 2002). Monthly volumes of consumptive use were then divided by the number of seconds in the month to get a daily rate. These daily crop consumptive use adjustments for each month for all regions of the State are shown in table 3.

5. Annual and monthly values for the 7 flow statistics for 254 stations were computed after their daily flow records were adjusted for crop consumptive use. The statistics for these stations in addition to 212 stations that did not need to be adjusted are shown in table 4.

Drainage Basin Characteristics

Climatic and physical characteristics of the drainage basins upstream of the streamflow-gaging stations selected for the study were used as independent variables in the regression equations to predict streamflow statistics. Using Geographic Information System (GIS) techniques, more than 30 different basin characteristics initially were computed for all 466 streamflow-gaging stations. The final selection of 21 basin characteristics that were used in the regression equations are described in table 5. Values of the 21 climatic and physical basin characteristics for all 466 streamflow-gaging stations are included in table 6. The computations were made using Arc Macro Language (AML) scripts run in ArcInfo, version 9.2 (Environmental Systems Research Institute, 2007). As listed in table 5, the basin characteristics were derived from various sources. Topographically related characteristics such as drainage area, elevation, relief, drainage density, and slope were computed using the National Hydrography Dataset Plus (NHD Plus) dataset, which was developed by the USGS and U.S. Environmental Protection Agency (EPA). NHD Plus includes a 30-meter Digital Elevation Model (DEM) combined with streamflow hydrography and other data layers (http://www.horizon-systems.com/NHDPlus/, accessed June 27, 2008). Climatic characteristics such as air temperature and precipitation were computed from datasets produced by the Parameter-elevation Regressions on Independent Slopes Model (PRISM) (http://www.prism.oregonstate.edu/, accessed June 27, 2008). Soil capacity and soil permeability characteristics were computed from the U.S. Natural Resources Conservation Service (NRCS) State Soil Geographic (STATSGO) datasets. Aquifer and geologic characteristics were computed from digitized published USGS maps (King and Beikman, 1974; McFarland, 1983; Gonthier, 1985). Forest cover was computed from the USGS National Land Cover Dataset (NLCD) (http://landcover.usgs.gov/natllandcover.php, accessed June 27, 2008).

Variable Adjustments

In regional regression studies, independent and dependent variables often need to be transformed into log space before the regression equation is created to ensure a linear relation between the independent and dependent variables. However, some independent and dependent variables for some stations had a value of zero that can not be logarithmically transformed. In such instances, a constant was added to the specific variable for all station data used in the equation.

The independent variables (climatic and physical characteristics of the drainage basins upstream of the streamflow-gaging stations) that sometimes had a value of zero were minimum slope, impervious area, forest cover, high-permeability geologic units, high-permeability aquifer units, and drainage density. A constant of 0.01 was used for forest cover, high-permeability geologic units, high-permeability aquifer units, and drainage density. A constant of 0.001 was used for minimum slope and impervious area, because most of the values for those variables were smaller than the values of the other variables.

To make the regression equation coefficients more balanced in magnitude, and thus more accurate, it was possible to adjust the magnitude of some of the independent variable data. An over-inflated coefficient commonly can occur if the minimum value in a variable's dataset is as large or larger than the maximum and minimum range of values for that variable. For this study, the annual maximum temperature (AXT) data for all 10 regions were decreased by 40 °F before they were transformed into log space and used to create the equations. Likewise, the annual minimum (ANT) and January maximum temperature (JXT) data for all 10 regions also were decreased by 20 °F before being transformed into log space.

The dependent variables (flow-duration and low-flow frequency statistics) also included some zeros at some streamflow-gaging stations. Although most of these stations were located in the east side of the study area, some of them also were located on small streams in the west side. Eighteen of the 466 streamflow-gaging stations had computed 95th percentile flow-duration flows that were zero. Four of these stations also had computed 50th percentile flow-duration flows that were zero. Many of the stations with zero value flow-durations statistics also had 7Q2 and 7Q10 statistics that were zero. As discussed previously, 52 of the 466 streamflow-gaging stations had one or more years of 7-day low flows that were zero. A conditional probability adjustment was used for these stations to compute the 7Q2 and 7Q10 statistics. If at least 50-percent of the 7-day annual values at a station were equal to zero, then the computed 7Q2 statistic for that station was set equal to zero. Likewise, if at least 10 percent of the 7-day annual values at a station were equal to zero, then the computed 7Q10 statistic for that station was set equal to zero.

Various approaches can be used to treat the zero values in a regression analysis depending on the number of streamflow-gaging stations in a dataset with dependent variables equal to zero. If the number of zero value dependent variables in the dataset are sufficient, it is possible to use logistic regression or a Tobit model (Tasker, 1989; Ludwig and Tasker, 1993; Kroll and Stedinger, 1999; Hortness, 2006). Kroll and Stedinger (1999) also evaluated the approach of adding a small constant value to all dependent variables in a dataset when there are one or more variables with a zero value. In their analysis, this approach was acceptable although not as preferable as using a Tobit model. For this study, the logistic regression and Tobit model approaches were not feasible because of an insufficient number of streamflow-gaging stations with zero value flow statistics for any single regional regression dataset. Some of the regression datasets contained only a single zero value station. Thus, adding a constant to all dependent variables in a dataset prior to the log transformation was a preferred approach. To determine an optimal constant for a dataset,

values of +0.01, +0.1, +1, or +10 were evaluated separately in the regression equations. The value that produced the highest R-squared and the lowest standard error was selected. All constants used in the final equations are shown in tables 7-16.

Modeling Regions

In a regional regression study, dividing a large study area into smaller more-homogeneous regions improves the accuracy of the regression equations. This is especially critical for study areas with the range of physical diversity of the Oregon landscape.

To determine if smaller regional datasets would produce more accurate regression equations, simple regression equations using the entire dataset of 466 of streamflow-gaging stations were created to predict the five flow-duration and two low-flow frequency statistics of the study. The equations used drainage area as their only input variable. By plotting the spatial distribution of positive and negative residuals from the regression equations, patterns helpful in dividing the study area into regions were identified (Richard M. Cooper, Oregon Water Resources Department, written commun. 2006). Figure 3 shows residuals from a simple regression equation that predicts the annual 7Q10 statistic. The residuals were computed as observed value minus predicted value. Although the figure does not show clearly defined regions within the study area, it is possible to see patterns of homogeneity that correspond with some of the EPA Level III ecoregions such as the *Coast Range*, *Willamette Valley*, *Cascade Range*, *Klamath Mountains*, and *Blue Mountains*.

Next, all 466 streamflow-gaging stations were overlain onto the EPA Level III ecoregion and 8-digit HUC data layers. The stations were then grouped into eight of the nine ecoregions that covered Oregon. The *Snake River Plain* ecoregion covers a fairly small portion of the State, and the few streamflow-gaging stations in that ecoregion were merged into the *Northern Basin and Range* ecoregion. The 8-digit HUCs of the streamflow-gaging stations also were used in the grouping criteria. If an 8-digit HUC was completely contained within an ecoregion, then all stations in that HUC were assigned to that ecoregion. However, if portions of an 8-digit HUC were in more than one ecoregion, the HUC and all stations located in that HUC were merged with the ecoregion that contained the greatest amount of area of the HUC.

Eight sets of simple regression models using drainage area as the only independent variable were used to evaluate the grouping of streamflow-gaging stations in the initial eight regions. An iterative process was used to reduce the regression equation error for each modeling region. Regional boundaries were adjusted until the errors in all the regression equations were minimized. When it was necessary to move stations from one ecoregion to another, all stations in a single 8-digit HUC were moved as a group in order to create more defined boundaries of the groups.

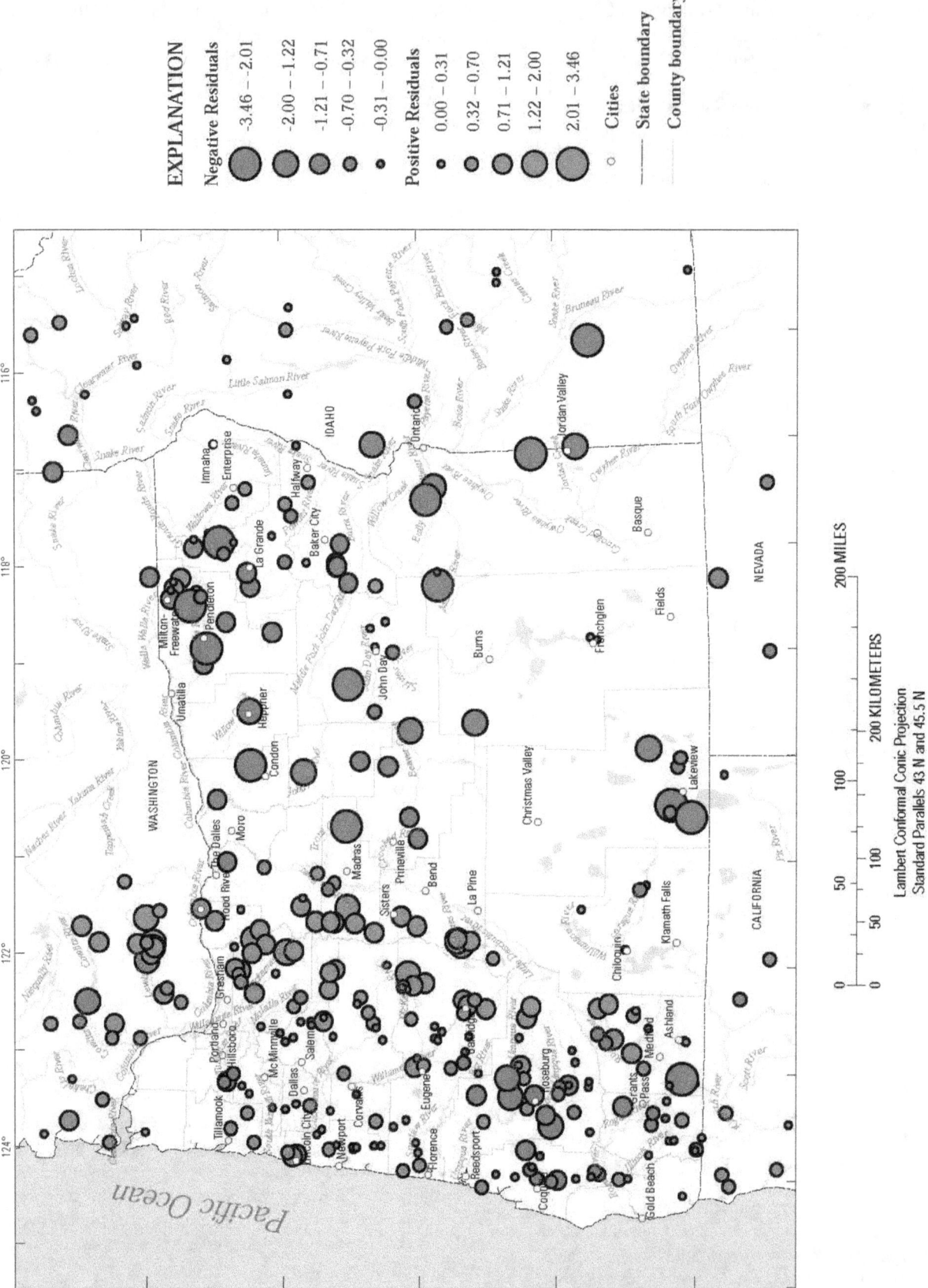

Figure 3.   Residuals of a simple 7Q10 regression equation for the entire study area.

During the iterative process of model testing and adjusting regional boundaries, it became apparent that the long narrow *Coast Range* group needed to be split near the middle to create a northern and a southern group. The split was made along an 8-digit HUC boundary. It also became apparent that the long narrow *Eastern Cascades Slopes and Foothills* region also should be similarly split into a northern and a southern group. The final 10 groups of stations were labeled as Regions 1 through 10 (fig. 4).

Independent Variable Selection

The selection of independent variables, or basin characteristics, for the regression equations in the 10 regions was determined using a combination of automated and manual techniques. Throughout the process, an effort was made to ensure that the independent variables had a hydrologic and physical basis to be used as predictors of the flow statistics. More than 30 basin characteristics initially were evaluated for each regression equation by creating and examining a cross correlation matrix of the log-transformed flow statistic and basin characteristics. Thus, some basin characteristics were removed from consideration as predictor variables if they had an extremely weak correlation with the flow statistic. A basin characteristic also was removed if the cross-correlation coefficient between it and other basin characteristics (with strong correlations to the flow statistic) was 0.6 or greater.

After the initial screening, the remaining basin characteristics were used to create a preliminary set of 910 regression equations for the entire study area. The equations were all created using Ordinary Least Squares forward and backward stepwise regression procedures included in the S-Plus program (Insightful Corporation, 2002). Stepwise regression is included in many statistical software packages and is a procedure that helps determine an optimal selection of independent variables for a multiple regression equation.

In a forward stepwise regression process, variables are added one by one. During each step, all unused variables are examined in order to determine which explains the largest amount of unexplained variation. After the addition of a variable, all variables selected are evaluated to ensure that each meets a predetermined level of significance in explaining the variation. Any variables found to be no longer significant are removed. These steps are repeated until none of the remaining unselected variables explain a significant amount of the remaining unexplained variation and all selected variables are significant.

In a backward stepwise regression, the procedure begins with all possible variables included in the equation. With each step, the least significant variable is eliminated. This step is repeated until all remaining variables in the equation are determined to be significant. A level of significance of 0.05 was used for the forward and backwards stepwise regressions.

The forward and backward stepwise regression analysis created two equations for each regression dataset. Sometimes, the two equations were identical, but generally the equation created by the backward stepwise regression method had more independent variables than the equation created by the forward stepwise regression method. A drawback in stepwise regression is that the created equations are not always optimal equations because not every possible combination of independent variables is evaluated. For example, variables that are eliminated at an early stage of backwards stepwise regression are not brought back to the equation. However, the results from the stepwise regression analysis were very useful as a guide in manually evaluating the independent variable selection for all regression equations. In addition to evaluating whether the independent variables made hydrologic sense, their signs were checked to ensure that they were used appropriately in the equation. For example, mean annual precipitation would be expected to have a positive relation with flow in an equation. As another rule, no more than four independent variables were used in an equation. Using too many independent variables when there is a limited number of stations can create an equation that "over-fits" the data. During the manual equation evaluation, the two main diagnostics that were checked included the coefficient of determination (R-squared) and the residual standard error. Higher values of the coefficient of determination generally are desirable in a regression analysis, especially when the dataset does not contain an outlier. An outlier can sometimes produce an inflated coefficient of determination that is significantly higher than the coefficient of determination that would result from a dataset that did not contain the outlier.

The most common independent variable that was used in almost all 910 equations was basin drainage area. The second most common variable was mean annual precipitation. On occasion, these two variables together produced the most optimal combination of variables for a regression equation.

Generalized-Least-Squares Regression Analysis

WLS and GLS have been used in regional regression studies because some of the assumptions in OLS with regards to equal weighting of the streamflow-gaging stations can be violated due to different lengths and variances of the annual flow series and cross correlation between different annual flow series. The feasibility of using either WLS and GLS for this study was evaluated with a software program developed by the USGS National Research Program (NRP) (Ken Eng, written commun., 2007). The program contains options for OLS, WLS, and GLS regression. The WLS and GLS algorithms were developed by Tasker (1980) and (Tasker and Stedinger, 1989), respectively. Required input for the NRP software program included independent and dependent variables and a time series of 7-day low-flow for each streamflow-gaging station. This data provided flow-record length, variance, and cross correlation information necessary to compute the

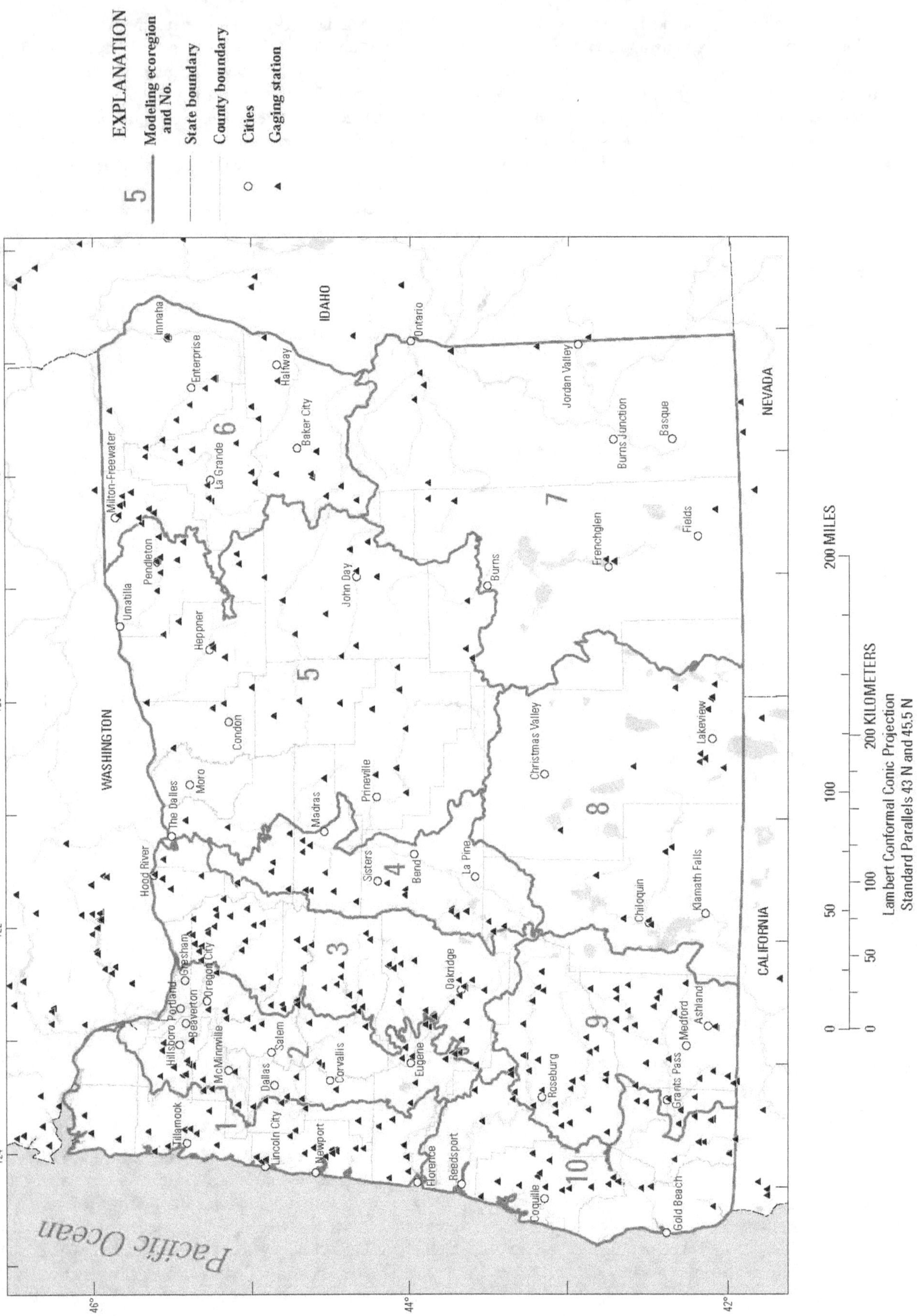

EXPLANATION

5 Modeling ecoregion and No.

State boundary

County boundary

○ Cities

▲ Gaging station

Figure 4. Ten modeling regions used for the regression equations.

station weights. A portion of the stations, especially in eastern Oregon, had one or more years in their annual series of 7-day low flows that were zero. In these instances, a constant value was added to each year's 7-day low-flow value for every station in the region. The constant, +0.01, +0.1 or +1.0, that was applied was the same one selected earlier in the OLS regression analysis when a constant value was added to the dependent variables in the dataset.

For WLS and GLS, output from the software developed by NRP included the equation coefficients, model error variance and the average variance of prediction (sum of the model and data-sampling errors), and a weighting matrix. The feasibility of using WLS or GLS for the low-flow frequency statistics was evaluated by testing a select number of regression equations, created earlier in OLS, from different regions of the study area. The differences in standard errors between the two methods generally were insignificant. A decision was made to use GLS for the low-flow frequency statistics because GLS computes streamflow-gaging station weights accounting for cross-correlation between the stations, varying flow-record lengths, and variances in the annual flows. The GLS regression equations were created using the same independent variables selected during the OLS regressions performed earlier using S-Plus. GLS coefficients generally closely matched those computed using OLS. Maximum discrepancies between the two methods appear in regions with high spatial correlation and greater residual error.

WLS or GLS could not be used to create regression equations for the flow-duration statistics. The formulation of the WLS or GLS weights requires an annual time series from each streamflow-gaging station in the dataset. The annual time series is needed to compute the variance of the station and the cross correlation of the station with other stations. Consequently, the final flow-duration regression equations were made using OLS.

Bias Correction Factors

As previously discussed, bias correction factors (BCF) were used to correct the bias present in retransformed logarithmic regression equations. Duan's (1983) smearing estimate technique was selected as an appropriate BCF to use for the flow-duration regression equations that were created using OLS regression. This BCF also has been used in other regional regression studies for OLS regression equations (Ries and Friesz, 2000; Flynn, 2003) and is computed from the following equation:

$$BCF_{Duan} = \frac{\sum_{i=1}^{n} 10^{e_i}}{n} \qquad (6)$$

where

BCF_{Duan} is the bias correction factor,

e_i is the regression residual, and

n is the number of streamflow-gaging stations in the regression.

Duan's (1983) smearing technique is not appropriate for the low-flow frequency regression equations because those equations were created using GLS regression. Because GLS regression uses a different method of computing the weighting matrix compared to OLS regression, the residuals have unequal weights (Flynn, 2003). The BCF coefficients for the low-flow frequency regression equations were computed using a technique described by Ferguson (1986) and Helsel and Hirsch (2002) as shown in the following equation:

$$BCF_{Ferguson} = \exp^{\left[0.5*\left(s^2\right)*5.302\right]} \qquad (7)$$

where

$BCF_{Ferguson}$ is the bias correction factor, and

S is the GLS regression standard error of prediction, in log units.

The computed BCF values for all flow-duration and low-flow frequency regression equations are listed in tables 7-16. The sample computations section illustrates how the BCF is used in the equations.

Final Regression Equations

Final regression equations for Regions 1-10 are listed in tables 7-16, along with dependent variable constants for zero values, bias correction factors, and performance metrics. Four performance metrics were used to evaluate the adequacy of the final regression equations:

- The **adjusted R-squared** *(R²adj)*, or the adjusted coefficient of determination, is a measure of the percentage of the variation explained by the independent variables of the model. The R^2 value is adjusted based on the degrees of freedom in the regression, thus penalizing models that use an excess number of independent variables. *R²adj* evaluates only the random error of predictions. Consequently, systematic errors such as a constant *bias* are not evaluated by *R²adj* (Lettenmaier and Wood, 1993).

- The **standard error of the estimate** (*SEE*, in log units and percent) measures the deviation between the measured and predicted data points. This error is reported for the flow-duration regression equations that were created using OLS. *SEE* is not appropriate for evaluating GLS regressions because unequal weighting given to the streamflow statistic at each station. The resulting unequally weighted residuals produce inflated *SEE* values that are not comparable to the *SEE* from an OLS analysis.

- The **standard error of the model** (*SEM*, in log units and percent) represents the error due to the model itself, and does not include sampling error. This error is only reported for the low-flow frequency regression equations that were created using GLS. *SEM* is the square root of the GLS model error variance described by Tasker and Stedinger (1989).

- The **standard error of the prediction** (*SEP*, in log units and percent) represents the sum of the model error and the sampling error. This error also is reported only for the low-flow frequency regression equations that were created using GLS. *SEP* is the square root of the GLS average variance of prediction described by Tasker and Stedinger (1989).

Prediction Intervals

The regression equations reported here predict the values of various streamflow characteristics. The true values of those characteristics remain unknown. Prediction intervals are a measure of the uncertainty associated with the prediction made by the regression equation. The interval is the predicted value plus and minus a margin of error. The margin of error is directly related to the certainty with which the predicted value is known. A prediction interval represents the probability that the true value of the characteristic will fall within the margin of error (Hirsch and others, 1993). For example, a prediction interval at the 90-percent confidence level means there is 90-percent chance the true value of characteristic will be within the margin of error. The margin of error includes both parameter uncertainty and the unexplained variability of the dependent variables.

Prediction intervals are automatically calculated at the 90-percent confidence level in the StreamStats program for all 910 regression equations that were developed from this study. Equations used to compute prediction intervals and correct for bias in StreamStats are from Tasker and Driver (1988) and are shown in the following:

$$\frac{1}{T} * \frac{Q_{estimate}}{BCF} < Q_{true} < T * \frac{Q_{estimate}}{BCF} \tag{8}$$

where

Q is the streamflow statistic,
BCF is the bias correction factor, and
T is computed as:

$$T = 10^{[t_{(\alpha/2, n-p)}(S_i)]} \tag{9}$$

where

$t_{(\alpha/2, n-p)}$ is the critical value of the student's t-distribution,
n is the number of stations in the regression equation,
p is the number of independent variables in the regression equation, and
S_i is computed as:

$$S_i = [MEV + X_i U X_i']^{0.5} \tag{10}$$

where

MEV is the model error variance from GLS or the error variance from OLS,
X_i is the row vector for the stream-gaging station i, starting with the number 1, followed by the logarithmic values of the basin variables used in the regression,
U is the covariance matrix from the regression, and
X_i' is the matrix algebra transpose of X_i.

Sample Computations

Example 1

The following is the estimate of the 50-percent flow-duration (*P50*) in January for Region 1.

Assume that an ungaged stream site of interest has a basin drainage area (*DA*) of 200 mi^2 and a mean annual precipitation (*P*) of 60 in/yr.

From table 7:

Log (*P50*) = -0.5732+0.9898*log(*DA*)+0.7616*log(*P*); therefore,

Log (*P50*) = 3.0586

P50 = 1,140 ft^3/s

The computed value is then adjusted using the BCF:

1,140 ft^3/s (1.016417) = 1,160 ft^3/s.

Example 2

The following is the estimate of the 7Q2 for August in Region 7.

Assume that an ungaged stream site of interest has a basin drainage area (*DA*) of 80 mi^2, mean annual precipitation (*P*) of 20 in/yr, and an annual maximum air temperature (*AXT*) of 58.0°F.

From table 13:

Log(1) + Log 7Q2 = 12.5176 + 0.7515*Log(*DA*) + 2.4953*Log(P) - 9.5375*Log(AXT)

Log(1)+ Log 7Q2 = 0.3755

1 + 7Q2= 2.37

7Q2 = 1.37 ft^3/s

A constant variable adjustment was applied to the computed value because the dependent variable dataset used to create the regression equation had one or more zero values.

The computed value is then adjusted using the BCF:

1.37 ft^3/s (1.075785) = 1.47 ft^3/s.

Accuracy and Limitations

In general, model accuracy tended to increase from the southeastern to northwestern regions of the study area from low-flow to high-flow conditions and from dry months to wet months. Based on equations for all 10 regions for annual and monthly flow statistics (a total of 130 values as indicated in tables 7-16), the standard errors of estimate of the high flow (5th percentile) and low flow (95th percentile) equations had medians of 42.4 and 64.4 percent, respectively. The adjusted coefficient of determination (R^2adj) of the 5th and 95th percentile equations had medians of 0.95 and 0.91, respectively. A similar pattern was seen in the low-flow frequency equations. The standard errors of prediction of the equations for the 7Q2 and 7Q10 statistics had medians of 51.7 and 61.2 percent, respectively. The adjusted coefficients of determination (R^2adj) of the 7Q2 and 7Q10 equations had medians of 0.94 and 0.92, respectively.

Use of the final regression equations should be limited to ungaged basins within Oregon in which the independent variables fall within the range of those sites used to develop the equations. The minimum and maximum values of all independent variables considered for each equation are shown in table 17. In addition, computations for independent variables at ungaged sites should be calculated using GIS datasets identical to those used in the study. StreamStats is populated with the same GIS datasets. If these equations are used at ungaged stream sites regulated by major reservoirs, or affected by significant diversions, they will produce estimates of natural unregulated flow conditions as opposed to actual flow conditions at those sites.

Many of the regression equations for locations in eastern Oregon are hampered by a sparser density of long-term streamflow stations, a high degree of streamflow variability, and a disproportionate amount of water use relative to streamflow. As such, careful consideration should be given to the prediction intervals when evaluating equation results for Regions 5-8, especially for low-flow equations. Depending on the level of accuracy needed, users should consider supplementing flow-statistic estimates made from the regression equations with estimates made using the drainage-area ratio, and partial-record site methods. Additional flow data collected from seepage runs along the stream upstream and downstream of the ungaged site of interest could provide an improved estimate of low-flow statistics (Riggs, 1972).

Data precision is decreased with regression equations that contain basin characteristics data created from GIS datasets. Computer generated tabular data typically are presented with arbitrary fixed decimal points. The precision of these data can not always be assumed. Final flow statistics estimated from regression equations that were created from measured flow data and GIS data should not be presented with a level of precision greater than 3 significant figures.

Summary and Conclusions

Techniques for estimating flow-duration and low-flow frequency statistics in unregulated streams throughout Oregon were developed in a cooperative study between the USGS and the Oregon Department of Transportation. Major components of the study included computing flow statistics at 466 active and inactive streamflow-gaging stations, computing climatic and physical basin characteristics at these stations, and developing regression equations to predict flow statistics at ungaged sites based on basin characteristics. The flow statistics included annual and monthly flow-duration quantiles for the 5th, 10th, 25th, 50th, and 95th percent exceedances and annual and monthly 7-day, 10-year (7Q10) and 7-day, 2-year (7Q2) low flows. Useful in characterizing a range of high- and low-flow conditions in Oregon streams, these statistics are of critical interest to Federal, State, and local agencies involved in activities such as water-quality regulation, biological habitat assessment, and water-supply planning and management. Low-flow statistics, for example, commonly are used as benchmarks when setting wastewater-treatment plant effluent limits and allowable pollutant loads to meet water-quality standards.

The study area, which included all of Oregon and adjacent areas of neighboring States, was divided into 10 regression modeling regions based on ecological, topographic, geologic, hydrologic, and climatic criteria. A total of 910 regression equations were created to estimate seven annual and monthly flow-duration and low-flow frequency statistics in all 10 regions. Equations to predict the five flow-duration statistics were created using Ordinary Least Squares regression. The standard error of estimate of the equations created to predict the high flow (5th percentile) and low flow (95th percentile) statistics had medians of 42.4 and 64.4 percent, respectively. The adjusted coefficient of determination (R^2adj) of the 5th and 95th percentile equations had medians of 0.95 and 0.91, respectively. Equations to predict the low-flow frequency statistics were created using Generalized Least Squares regression. The standard error of prediction of the equations created to predict the 7Q2 and 7Q10 statistics had medians of 51.7 and 61.2 percent, respectively. The adjusted coefficient of determination (R^2adj) of the 7Q2 and 7Q10 equations had medians of 0.94 and 0.92, respectively.

The regression equations created in the study are not intended to be used at ungaged sites in which the basin characteristics are outside of the range of those used to create the regression equations. Flow statistics predicted by the equations represent natural unregulated flow conditions in Oregon. If the equations are used at ungaged sites on streams regulated by reservoirs or affected by water-supply and agricultural withdrawals, then the estimate would need to be adjusted if actual flow conditions are of interest.

All 910 regression equations developed for this study are included in the USGS StreamStats Web-based tool (http://water.usgs.gov/osw/streamstats/index.html, accessed August 29, 2007). StreamStats provides users with a set of both annual and monthly flow-duration and low-flow frequency estimates for ungaged sites within Oregon in addition to the basin characteristics for the sites. Prediction intervals at the 90-percent confidence level also are automatically computed. A prediction interval at the 90-percent confidence level means that there is 90-percent assurance that the true value of a flow statistic at an ungaged site will be within a plus or minus interval around the predicted flow statistic.

Acknowledgments

This study was funded by the Oregon Department of Transportation. The authors thank Mathew Mabey of the Oregon Department of Transportation who made this study possible.

The authors also thank:

* Richard Cooper and Ken Stahr, Oregon Department of Water Resources, who provided data for the study and reviewed this report.

* Kernell Ries, USGS Maryland Water Science Center, for his guidance and assistance in regional regression low-flow statistics.

* David Lorenz, USGS Minnesota Water Science Center, for his assistance in using the S-Plus statistical software package.

References Cited

Berenbrock, C., 2002, Estimating the magnitude of peak flows at selected recurrence intervals for streams in Idaho: U.S. Geological Survey Water-Resources Investigations Report 02-4170, 59 p.

Butler, E., Reid, J.K., and Berwick, V.K., 1966, The Great Basin, Part 10 of Magnitude and frequency of floods in the United States: U.S. Geological Survey Water-Supply Paper 1684, 256 p.

Cooper, R.M., 2002, Determining surface-water availability in Oregon: State of Oregon Water Resources Department Open-File Report SW 02-002, 157 p.

Cooper, R.M., 2005, Estimation of peak discharges for rural, unregulated streams in western Oregon: U.S. Geological Survey Scientific Investigations Report 2005-5116, 134 p.

Cooper, R.M., 2006, Estimation of peak discharges for rural, unregulated streams in eastern Oregon: Oregon Water Resources Department Open-File Report SW 02-002, Salem, Oregon, 57 p.

Cuenca, R.H., Nuss, J.L., MartinezCob, A., Katul, G.G., and FaciGonzalez, J.M., 1992, Oregon crop water use and irrigation requirements: Corvallis, Oregon State University Agricultural Experiment Station and Extension Service, Extension Miscellaneous Publication 8530, 184 p.

Duan, N., 1983, Smearing estimate: A nonparametric retransformation method: Journal of the American Statistical Association, v. 78, no. 383, p. 605-610.

Environmental Systems Research Institute, Inc. (ESRI), 2007, ArcInfo version 9.2, accessed July 1, 2008, at http://webhelp.esri.com/arcgisdesktop/9.2

Ferguson, R.I., 1986, River loads underestimated by rating curves: Water Resources Research, v. 22, no. 1, p. 74-76.

Flynn, R.H., 2003, Development of regression equations to estimate flow durations and low-flow frequency statistics, *in* New Hampshire streams: U.S. Geological Survey Water-Resources Investigations Report 02-4298, 66 p.

Gannett, M.W., Lite, K.E., LaMarche, J.L., Fisher, B.J., and Polette, D.J., 2007, Ground-water hydrology of the upper Klamath Basin, Oregon and California: U.S. Geological Survey Scientific Investigations Report 07-5050, 84 p.

Gonthier, J.B., 1985, A description of aquifer units in eastern Oregon: U.S. Geological Survey Water-Resources Investigations Report 84-4095, 39 p.

Grygier, J.C., Stedinger, J.R., and Yin, Hong-Bin, 1989, A generalized maintenance of variance extension procedure for extending correlated series: Water Resources Research, v. 25, no. 3, p. 345–349.

Harris, D.D., and Hubbard, L.E., 1983, Magnitude and frequency of floods in eastern Oregon: U.S. Geological Survey Water-Resources Investigations Report 82-4078, 39 p.

Harris, D.D., Hubbard, L.L., and Hubbard, L.E., 1979, Magnitude and frequency of floods in western Oregon: U.S. Geological Survey Open-File Report 79-553, 29 p.

Helsel, D.R., and Hirsch, R.M., 2002, Statistical methods in water resources: U.S. Geological Survey Techniques of Water-Resources Investigations, book 4, chap. A3, 510 p.

Hirsch, R.M., 1982, A comparison of four streamflow record extension techniques: Water Resources Research, v. 18, no. 4, p. 1081–1088.

Hirsch, R.M., Helsel, D.R., Cohn, T.A., and Gilroy, E.J., 1993, Statistical treatment of hydrologic data, *in* Maidmont, D.R., ed., Handbook of Hydrology: New York, McGraw-Hill, p. 17.1–17.55.

Hortness, J.E., 2006, Estimating low-flow frequency statistics for unregulated streams in Idaho: U.S. Geological Survey Scientific Investigations Report 2006-5035, 31 p.

Hulsing, H., and Kallio, N.A., 1964, Pacific slope basins in Oregon and lower Columbia River basin, Part 14 of Magnitude and frequency of floods in the United States: U.S. Geological Survey Water-Supply Paper 1689, 320 p.

Insightful Corporation, 2002, S-PLUS Version 6.1 for Windows Professional Edition, Release 1: Copyright, Lucent Technologies, Inc.

King, P.B., and Beikman, H.M., 1974, Explanatory text to accompany the geologic map of the United States: U.S. Geological Survey Professional Paper 902, 40 p.

Kjelstrom, L.C., 1998, Methods for estimating selected flow-duration and flood-frequency characteristics at ungaged sites in central Idaho: U.S. Geological Survey Water-Resources Investigations Report 94-4120, 10 p.

Kroll, C.N., and Stedinger, J.R., 1999, Development of regional regression relationships with censored data: Water Resources Research, v. 35, no. 3, p. 775-784.

Lettenmaier, D.P., and Wood, E.F., 1993, Hydrological Forecasting, Chapter 26, in Maidment, D., ed., Handbook of Hydrology: Columbus, Ohio, McGraw-Hill, 30 p.

Ludwig, R.H., and Tasker, G.D., 1993, Regionalization of low-flow characteristics of Arkansas streams: U.S. Geological Survey Water-Resources Investigations Report 93-4013, 32 p.

Lystrom, D.J., 1970, Evaluation of the flow-data program in Oregon: U.S. Geological Survey Open-File Report, 29 p.

Manga, M., 1996, Hydrology of spring-dominated streams in the Oregon Cascades: Water Resources Research, v. 32, no. 8, p. 2435-2439.

McFarland, W.D., 1983, A description of aquifer units in Western Oregon: U.S. Geological Survey Open-File Report 82-165, 43 p.

Parrett, C., and Johnson, D.R., 2004, Methods for estimating flood frequency in Montana based on data through year 1998: U.S. Geological Survey Water-Resources Investigations Report 03-4308, 101 p., 1 pl.

Ries, K.G., 1994, Estimation of low-flow duration discharges in Massachusetts: U.S. Geological Survey Water-Supply Paper 2418, 50 p.

Ries, K.G., and Friesz, P.J., 2000, Methods for estimating low-flow statistics for Massachusetts streams: U.S. Geological Survey Water-Resources Investigations Report 00-4135, 81 p.

Riggs, H.C., 1972, Low-flow investigations: U.S. Geological Survey Techniques of Water-Resources Investigations, book 4, chap. B1, 18 p.

Risley, J.C., and Laenen, A., 1999, Upper Klamath Lake Basin nutrient-loading study—Assessment of historic flows in the Williamson and Sprague Rivers: U.S. Geological Survey Water-Resources Investigations Report 98-4198, 22 p.

Searcy, J.K., 1959, Flow-duration curves, Manual of hydrology—Part 2. Low-flow techniques: U.S. Geological Survey Water-Supply Paper 1542-A, 33 p.

Stedinger, J.R., and Thomas, W.O., Jr., 1985, Low-flow frequency estimation using base-flow measurements: U.S. Geological Survey Open-File Report 85-95, 22 p.

Tasker, G.D., 1980, Hydrologic regression with weighted least squares: Water Resources Research, v. 16, no. 6, p. 1107-1113.

Tasker, G.D., 1989, Regionalization of low flow characteristics using logistic and GLS regression, in Kavvas, M.L., ed., New directions for surface water modeling: IAHS Publication 181, p. 323-331.

Tasker, G.D., and Driver, N.E., 1988, Nationwide regression models for predicting urban runoff water quality at unmonitored sites: Water Resources Bulletin, v. 24, no. 5, p. 1091-1101.

Tasker, G.D., and Stedinger, J.R., 1989, An operational GLS model for hydrologic regression: Journal of Hydrology, v. 111, p. 361-375.

Thomas, B.E., Hjalmerson, H.W., and Waltemeyer, S.D., 1993, Methods for estimating magnitude and frequency of floods in the southwestern United States: U.S. Geological Survey Open-File Report 93-419, 211 p.

Thomas, C.A., Broom, H.C., and Cummans, J.E., 1963, Snake River basin, Part 13 of Magnitude and frequency of floods in the United States: U.S. Geological Survey Water-Supply Paper 1688, 250 p.

U.S. Environmental Protection Agency, 1996, Level III ecoregions of the continental United States: Corvallis, Oregon, National Health and Environmental Effects Research Laboratory Map M-1, various scales.

U.S. Interagency Advisory Committee on Water Data, 1982, Guidelines for determining flood flow frequency: Reston, Virginia, U.S. Geological Survey, Office of Water Data Coordination, Hydrology Committee Bulletin 17B, 183 p.

Vogel, R.M., and Stedinger, J.R., 1985, Minimum variance streamflow record augmentation procedures: Water Resources Research, v. 21, no. 5, p. 715–723.

Young, L.E., and Cruff, R.W., 1967, Pacific Slope Basins in California, Part 11, Vol. 2, of Magnitude and frequency of floods in the United States: U.S. Geological Survey Water-Supply Paper 1686, 308 p.

This page left intentionally blank

Tables

Tables 1-17 are provided in a Microsoft® Excel workbook, which can be accessed at http://pubs.usgs.gov/sir/2008/5126/ sir20085126_tables.xls.

Table 1.   Description of streamflow-gaging stations used in regression equations for estimating flow-duration and low-flow frequency statistics in Oregon.

Table 2.   Selection of streamflow-gaging stations and their number of years of record used in the annual and monthly regression equations for estimating flow-duration and low-flow frequency statistics in Oregon.

Table 3.   Monthly consumptive-use adjustments.

Table 4.   Annual and monthly flow duration and low-flow frequency statistics for each streamflow-gaging station used in the regression equations.

Table 5.   Description of basin characteristics used in regression equations to predict flow-duration and low-flow frequency statistics in Oregon.

Table 6.   Basin characteristics for the streamflow-gaging stations used in the regression equations.

Table 7.   Regression analysis results for estimating flow-duration and low-flow frequency statistics based on data from Region 1.

Table 8.   Regression analysis results for estimating flow-duration and low-flow frequency statistics based on data from Region 2.

Table 9.   Regression analysis results for estimating flow-duration and low-flow frequency statistics based on data from Region 3.

Table 10.   Regression analysis results for estimating flow-duration and low-flow frequency statistics based on data from Region 4.

Table 11.   Regression analysis results for estimating flow-duration and low-flow frequency statistics based on data from Region 5.

Table 12.   Regression analysis results for estimating flow-duration and low-flow frequency statistics based on data from Region 6.

Table 13.   Regression analysis results for estimating flow-duration and low-flow frequency statistics based on data from Region 7.

Table 14.   Regression analysis results for estimating flow-duration and low-flow frequency statistics based on data from Region 8.

Table 15.   Regression analysis results for estimating flow-duration and low-flow frequency statistics based on data from Region 9.

Table 16.   Regression analysis results for estimating flow-duration and low-flow frequency statistics based on data from Region 10.

Table 17.   Maximum and minimum values of basin characteristics used in the regression equations.